IN RETAIL
Jeremy Dixon

ΛRΛ<HN€ PR€$$

Jeremy Dixon, poem by poem, every day, tries to make morning of mourning, entering our pain as sellers and customers, creating a humane custom—an absolute virtue of putting things back exactly where you found it. If we really must adhere to 'uniform and appearances rules,' these poems beautifully discern an ostentation somehow even in that capricious regularity. Dixon reminds us that poems restore desire, that they seek transgression, that they discover their own forms, and dares the reader as a kind of store detective to search our lines more. There we will find the real work being done.

Al Filreis

Jeremy Dixon's collection is a delicious inventory of the interaction between people and objects on shelves. His writing shows precision, humility and compassion for shoppers and fellow-staff who struggle to navigate a world in which souls are bought and sold. This is an elegant portrait of a world little celebrated in poetry, original in insight and form.

Gwyneth Lewis

Jeremy Dixon's astute unflinching observations of life in a well-known high street chemist brilliantly illustrate the experience of working in such a setting. We've all been customers, but how many of us have experienced the other side of the till? In Retail brings home with humour and compassion the annoying absurdities of working for a large corporation, and trying to please the ever-varying public. How do you address a customer after hours of repeating the same phrases over and over? There's the recognisably distorted voice on the tannoy pronounced 'far too soft' and the customer announcement, 'is there anyone here in charge?' The security guard carrying an 'Opium gift set' and 'peering through the L'Oréal stacks at a known thief'. The customer who simply has to confide, 'oh I swore I wouldn't say/ anything to anyone', and the 'minor reality face/wearing a black beanie' are all too familiar. You will discover and recognise so much about life in the here and now in Jeremy Dixon's range of subtle, poignant and captivating poems.

Julie-ann Rowell

First published in UK 2019 by Arachne Press Limited
100 Grierson Road, London SE23 1NX
www.arachnepress.com
© Jeremy Dixon 2019
ISBN: 978-1-909208-72-8

Page design © Cherry Potts 2019
Thanks to Muireann Grealy for her proofing.
Printed on wood-free paper in the UK by TJ International,
Padstow.

Acknowledgements

I am very grateful to the editors of the following publications in which some of these poems (or versions of them) first appeared: *Eye Socket Journal, Lighthouse Journal, Really System* and the Arachne Press anthology *The Other Side of Sleep*. An earlier form of this series was long-listed for the *Cinnamon Press Poetry Award* and also printed as a limited-edition artist's book by *Hazard Press*.

I would also like to thank the many people who have encouraged and supported me in the writing of this book: the Chapter Eleven gang (Marc Evans, Bernard John, Katrina Kirkwood, Griff Taylor), Ivy Alvarez, Julie-ann Rowell, and especially my editor Cherry Potts.

Finally, this book would not exist without the beneficial influences of my mother, father and sister, and of my Gitananda Yoga and ModPo families.

Introduction

This collection is the result of my part-time job in a well-known chain of chemists, which rather unexpectedly turned out to be a great source of poetic inspiration.

Most of the poems in this book began life as hurried lines scribbled on the back of a length of till roll in the lull between sales. As staff members were not allowed to carry any personal items while on the shop-floor, I hid these scraplets in my sock and prayed that today wasn't the surprise-spot-search-in-the-store-cupboard day.

This book is dedicated to all my former colleagues and customers and to everything that I learned from them.

We're SHOPPING, we're shopping
Pet Shop Boys

{STAFFED}

00/01

With the night come drunks
from the Bay wanting
Red Bull and paracetamol,

who swear when the till
won't sell them five packs.
Come methadone paper

wavers, talking backwards,
crashing electric doors.
Come red raw builders

buying aerosol plasters,
their Pepsi kids swerving
Perfume on scooters.

Five minutes to go
and a bulldogged woman
is after some discount

Revlon foundation. All there is
is a labelled gap. She leans close
to whisper: *I can get you cut.*

00/02

I've won an Armani Homme tester
for being the pinkest assistant at today's
mega-points bonus event. I wear a pink
shirt and a pink tie bought cheap in Oxfam
Penarth. The Beauty girls sport pink tops
with pink skirts, pink tights and pink shoes,
flick aerosol-sprayed pink hair,
pink glitter irritating eyes an all-day red.
So when my victory is announced
it's not a surprise to hear a low rumble
from the make-up counter. And I bet
it didn't help me writing an acceptance
speech on the staffroom flipchart
making out I'd been handed an Oscar.

00/03

Good morning.
Do you have an Advantage Card?
And would you like a bag?
Please enter your PIN.

Good morning.
Thank you for waiting.
Do you have an Advantage Card?
And would you like a bag?
Please enter your PIN.

Good morning.
Thank you for waiting.
No one's answering the bell.
Do you have an Advantage Card?
And would you like a bag?
Please enter your PIN.

Good morning.
Thank you for waiting.
No one's answering the bell.
They're all at a meeting without me.
Do you have an Advantage Card?
And would you like a bag?
Please enter your PIN.

Good morning.
Thank you for waiting.
No one's answering the bell.
They're all at a meeting without me.
Seems I'm the only one left in the shop.
Do you have an Advantage Card?
And would you like a bag?
Please enter your PIN.

Good morning.
Thank you for waiting.
No one's answering the bell.
They're all at a meeting without me.
Seems I'm the only one left in the shop.
I could find myself with a riot on my hands.
Do you have an Advantage Card?
And would you like a bag?
Please enter your PIN.

Morning.
Thank you for waiting.
No one's answering the bell.
They're all at a party without me.
Seems I'm the only one left in the ship.
I could find myself with a riot on my hands.
Yes, you're right it isn't good enough is it.
Did you have an Advantage Card?
And would you like a bag?
Please enter your PIN.

Mourning.
Thank you for belling.
No one's answering the weight.
And there's another party without me.
Seems I'm the only one left in the world.
I could find myself with blood on my hands.
Yes, you're right it isn't God enough is it.
Mother says contactless is Satan's kiss.
Have you taken the advantage?
And do you need a nosebag?
Please enter your PAIN.

00/04

a minor reality face
wearing a black beanie
pulled down tight to hide

his TV quiff is rumoured
in the queue for Pharmacy
excited we circle Vitamins

pretending to pull forward
gossiping close to spy his meds
and rate him out of ten

on my life and
no word of a freaking lie
he was cowing lush like

00/05

That's my voice on the Tannoy
doing the end of day:
This store will close in ten minutes

so please make your way
to the tills at the front
of the shop to pay. Except when

I release the blue button Suzie
Dispenser says it was far too soft
and garbled, nobody understood.

00/06

Natalie can hear a man
humming beneath
the back shop stairs

only it's 10pm and
apart from the Pharmacist
we're the only ones in

00/07

Seems we all get headaches.
There used to be a staff
stash of paracetamol
kept behind Pharmacy
but now you have to buy
your own. Meena says
there is nothing between
a sixteen or a forty-two
pence box, different brands
but the same manufacturer.
Just buy the cheapest
she shouts across
a waiting wheelchair.

00/08

the Late team is working extra duty
sales-planning Christmas in mid-September
obeying lasered maps of where to stack

Lipsy and Jamie Oliver
the shelves are filthy
far too low for packs to stand

Upside Down plays on the radio
and I attempt an electric slide
but they're too young to appreciate an 80s move

behind the tills are baskets of returns
no-one has noticed
they will still be here tomorrow

00/09

somewhere swaying through CCTV
is me on top of a stockroom ladder
balanced between racks of Ted Baker

my right heel tucked
into my left thigh
palms together at the chest

showing Abbie what Vriksasana is
only she hates heights
and has her eyes shut

00/10

This is a customer announcement:
Would a member of Beauty go to hell.

This is a customer announcement:
Put that back exactly where you found it.

This is a customer announcement:
La la la. La la la la la. La la la. La la la la la.

This is a customer announcement:
Don't you have anything else better to do?

This is a customer announcement:
We cannot afford security.

This is a customer announcement:
It is illegal to photograph labels.

This is a customer announcement:
Is there anyone here in charge?

This is a customer announcement:
He's with somebody else right now.

This is a customer announcement:
Who just punched the panic alarm?

SILENCE = DEATH

00/11

I think that relief sales assistant
just winked at me through a wire

cage of Champney's better-than-
half-price offer-of-the-week

but I can't be sure he looks
incredibly young and it could have

been a twitch the air conditioning
can sometimes get you that way

00/12

only don't tell anyone I told you oh
I can't believe I've just told you

oh I swore I wouldn't say
anything to anyone

it's supposed to be
totally hush-hush

no one is supposed to know
everyone thinks he's a girlfriend

00/13

the in-store radio is on a major seventies kick
after an advert for Snoxin anti-wrinkle serum
You Make Me Feel (Mighty Real) starts

replaying a dark corner of the youth club
where I dance by myself to Sylvester
unable to resist that immaculate beat

compelled to leave the false safety
of a line of canvas chairs
failing to see what is apparent

to everyone else
watching me

punched the length of the pool table

{MANAGED}

00/14

If large groups gathered
in the car park cause concern

alarm doors and lower front
shutters. If time allows

unlock fragrance cabinets
bank takings upstairs

and let Nottingham know.
Exit by the rear fire escape.

00/15

would it be wrong to say
how the safes work
how you need two people
each with an eight-digit code

(most likely their birthday)
to unlock the safe on the left
containing a key for the right
or how on a Monday morning

they will hold seven clear bags
of last week's takings
that in the countdown to Christmas
can add up to over 100 grand

just awaiting lunchtime collection
by a solitary security guard
who sometimes on his long walk
stops off in the staff toilets

or even how those magnetic
limpets are deceptively loose
but will only trigger alarms
if you dare to move them too fast

00/16

by wig
by stick
by silence

by spouse
by gay
by job

by dog
by credit
by manners

by pennies
by chocolate
by stink

by puke
by purse
by mud

by Welsh
by age
by twitch

by bringing Marigold gloves to pack yourself

00/17

As from Monday all staff must adhere
to new uniform and appearance rules
Kris can't wear his silver watch anymore
they have had a word: ostentatious

00/18

they continue their important calls
repeat too often the name on your badge

they hire a ridiculous costume
tell you you're playing Santa Claus

they ask if you're the Manager
if you sell any cream that prolongs

they end Carol's contract early for
refusing an extra New Year's shift

they sneer at the offer of a plastic bag
want to pay thirty-two pence with a credit card

they call you an imbecile who can't do their job

00/19

Date Check Drinks
Date Check Crisps
Date Check Hair
Date Check Pain
Date Check Skin
Date Check Christmas
Date Check Weight
Date Check Baby's
Date Check Men's
Date Check Gum
Date Check Sun
Date Check Stars
Date Check Open
Date Check Lunch
Date Check Close
Date Check Last
Date Check Next
Date Check Now
Date Check Date
Date Check Tick
Date Check Signature

00/20

in the pyramid of being best
for Customer Care there are
three grades: not-performing
performing and legendary
(or UNICORN we call it)

there are rumours that quotas
are fixed in advance so anyone
could be told you're as bad
as the boy never here or she
who walks away from queues

so we worry what level
each other has met and
do they deserve extra and
should their pay remain the same
frozen for another year

00/21

A huge fuss was made of just
how wonderful the quality
of this year's Christmas Temp
applications was. Three fabs
were hired to start the following
Monday. Only one turned up.

00/22

an informal not-going-
on-your-record-yet threat
of formal disciplinary proceedings

for failing to spot an out-
of-date pack of Shapers de-cored
crunchy apple snack is what

prompted my resignation
locked in the safe room
at 8.30am on a Bank Holiday

well that and being told I couldn't
swap shifts for the Small Publishers' Fair
because I was never as fast as Jill or Gill

{CONSUMED}

00/23

most Thursday lunchtimes
inspiration appears
always

grabs one bag
of yoghurt-
dipped

banana chips pays
with warm
change

00/24

in distant
corners of
the car park
boys sit in
cars smoking
every window
wound up

00/25

did he know
who I was

when he asked
how I was

how my dad was
and I told him

how he was
when he asked

and I told him
did I know

who he was
did he know

today the queue is strung with angry people
angry that we are leaving
angry that people are angry that we are leaving
angry that people are still talking about leaving
angry at Cameron
angry at Farage
angry at MPs
angry at AMs
angry at Labour
angry at Plaid
angry at their parents
angry at the Papers
angry at the Pound
angry that all the Star Gifts sold out before they arrived

00/27

I know who the store detective is,
overheard him outside Argos
report an offender to the Bill.
Then he came in for a meal deal

and paid with a staff discount card.
Now I see him all the time,
a tall man carrying an Opium gift-set
cruising Rimmel London and Barry M,

peering through the L'Oréal stacks
at a known thief, whose mug shot
is on the shrink wall in the back shop,
haloed with red exclamation marks.

00/28

the omi from Pets at Home next door
buys two Diet Cokes on promotion
it's hard not to stare at his chest
Stop me & ask about ticks & fleas

00/29

A man buys a pint of milk
And I'm not buying anything else,
because I've been so bad lately.
Really bad.
Really, really bad.
So bad.
So very bad.
Bad. Bad.
So really, really bad.

00/30

Pear Drops
in a Jar
for Cerys
Boxers
for David
& Jason
White sports
Maybelline
Volume
Express
Potatoes
Yorkshires
Frozen Veg
Peanuts
for Stockings

00/31

scrub a receipt
fool the till

slip lipstick
in a sock

cram four packs into one
fill a pram

wear two jackets
never bring identity

say it came
from Asda

have friends outside
with a van

shout loud
threaten scare

00/32

your exclusive Miss Dior
50ml couture set with a slight dent
to the embossed lower left-hand corner

was only an hour before
wrestled from the coat
of a furious teenager

00/33

most men
won't wait
for one
penny change

00/34

please can I have an iphone X
please can I have an Xbox One
please can I have Hexbugs
please can I have Hot Wheels
please can I have a black wollit
please can I have how
please can I have Portmeirion
please can I have to listen
please can I have a first edition
please can I have Thom Gunn
please can I have not this
please can I have tight ropes
please can I have no interview
please can I have fixed margins
please can I have transgressions
please can I have the arena
please can I have them back
please can I have please

00/35

three of us in a cupboard by the chillers
surrounded by CCTV
a broken desk fan and
two blister packs of Gillette Fusion

fifty minutes wanting
no eye contact
with a guy in striped boxers
jeans at his knees

daring the store detective
to search him more
I give him a tissue
for his sweating neck

the police arrive
return me to the queue
fingers shake as I count out change
for people who don't know

00/36

you're in pyjamas screaming
through the late-night hatch
it's Christmas Eve someone
is dying in your front room

ABOUT ARACHNE PRESS

Arachne Press is a micro publisher of (award-winning!) short story and poetry anthologies and collections, novels including a Carnegie Medal nominated young adult novel, and a photographic portrait collection.

We are expanding our range all the time, but the short form is our first love. We keep fiction and poetry live, through readings, festivals (in particular our Solstice Shorts Festival), workshops, exhibitions and all things to do with writing.

Follow us on Twitter:
@ArachnePress
@SolShorts

Like us on Facebook:
ArachnePress
SolsticeShorts2014